PATCHWORK

FROM BEGINNER TO EXPERT

PATCHWORK

FROM BEGINNER TO EXPERT

JENNY BULLEN

B.T. Batsford Ltd, London

© Jenny Bullen

First published 1992

Typeset by J&L Composition Ltd, Filey, North Yorkshire
Printed in Singapore

Published by B.T. Batsford Ltd
4 Fitzhardinge Street, London W1H OAH

British Library Cataloguing-in-Publication Data. A catalogue record for this book is available from the British Library.

ISBN 0 7134 6651 0

ACKNOWLEDGEMENTS

I should like to thank Jim Pascoe for all the photographs that appear in this book. I should also like to thank all those students and friends who generously provided much of the work photographed, in particular Sandra Hoult, Diana Mitchell and Ann Ohlenschlager.

Page 1   *Panel using patchwork as a design source. Hand-dyed silk patches glued to a background and held in place with stitchery. Silk and paper patches are used in the border.* (Anne Coleman)

Page 3   *The design for this quilt was influenced by Indian patchwork. It is in strong, plain colours and has been hand-quilted in a variety of coloured threads so that the quilting pattern plays an important part in the surface design.* (Jean Draper)

CONTENTS

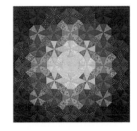

INTRODUCTION

PATCHWORK is a fairly inexpensive and simple craft. All you need is basic sewing equipment and an assortment of fabrics. But beware — it soon becomes addictive, and you will find it impossible to pass fabric or patchwork shops without pausing to inspect the latest supplies!

FABRICS

There are specialist patchwork shops all over the country, selling cottons and polyester/cotton blends in all colours, plain and prints. Many of these are imported from the United States. Departments in large stores also sell a wide variety of fabrics. If you are a complete beginner, it is worth paying a visit to one of these shops to buy two or three ½–metre lengths — choose shades of one colour and include a plain fabric as well as prints. With these, you will be able to work through most of the techniques described in this book.

Jumble sales are often a good source of fabrics, but you must wash any secondhand fabric carefully and inspect it for wear and fading. Anything that shows any sign of wear should be used with great caution.

All fabrics should be washed carefully by hand and pressed before you begin. There is usually some shrinkage and strong colours will 'bleed' slightly, especially the reds. It is worth putting a little household salt into the rinsing water. American fabrics seem to bleed more than those fabrics manufactured under British names; they also have more

(Above) *A small selection of the variety of fabrics suitable for patchwork.*

(Right) *An assortment of different fabrics have been used in this wall hanging with a design of polar bears. Machine-pieced and hand-quilted.* (Valerie McCallum)

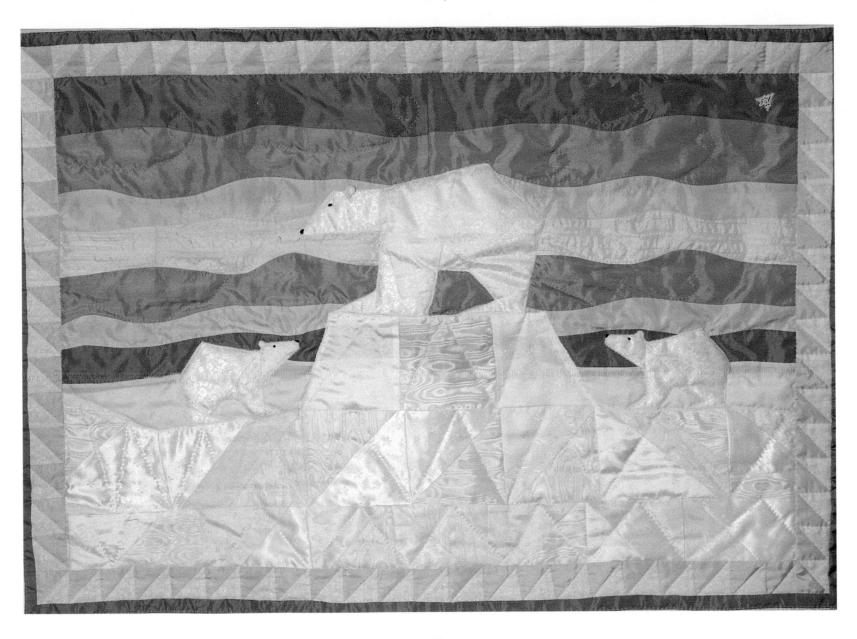

of a tendency to fade in strong sunlight, so bear this in mind when choosing your fabrics.

Pure cotton is a joy to work with: it creases easily, can be ironed and generally behaves well. Polyester/cottons are not quite so easy to handle: they will not crease as easily as pure cottons, but they are worth investigating, nonetheless. If you use polyester/cottons, 50/50 blends are probably best.

Silks create a luxurious, exotic effect and when they are quilted deep shadows are formed. They are not, however, very easy to work with: they do not have the natural 'stretch' of cottons and they fray easily. Creases, pin marks and water marks are difficult to remove. If you are working with small silk patches, it helps to iron them on to a lightweight Vilene. It is also better to tack work than to use too many pins; in any case, remove all tacking and pins as soon as possible.

If you intend to make a quilt or cushions that will require a great deal of washing, then cotton or cotton blends are ideal. However, if, as I hope you will, you intend to experiment with patchwork, then absolutely any fabric can be used, from pure cottons to fine silks, velvets and every kind of manmade fibre.

There are one or two points of which you should be aware. A lot of fabrics are not as tolerant as cottons when ironed. Some will not, for instance, take a very hot iron and it is always advisable to use a pressing cloth or you may find unwelcome iron marks on your fabrics. If you are mixing fabrics in a piece of work, heavier fabrics such as velvets will be difficult to handle when placed next to fine silks.

If you intend to dye your fabrics, some manmade fibres will not accept the dyes. Habotai silk, although it will dye beautifully, is especially difficult to handle — 'runs' are inclined to appear each time a needle is inserted in the fabric.

COLOUR

Whatever you intend to make, whether it is a small cot quilt or a large double bed quilt, cushions or a wall hanging, colour is very important. However well planned, designed and put together, if the patchwork does not 'sparkle' the whole effect will be ruined. Most people have an inbuilt colour sense and it must be remembered that one person's colour scheme will not be to everyone's liking.

These days, patchwork fabrics are often sold in ranges of one colour and it is a relatively simple matter to find five or six fabrics that will 'go' together. However, if you exhibit your work you may find that there will be several almost identical patchwork quilts at the same exhibition. With a little knowledge of basic colour theory and the courage to experiment, your work will soon become unique to you.

COLOUR THEORY

The three primary colours are red, yellow and blue.

If two of these colours are mixed together, a secondary colour is created (Fig 1 overleaf):

> red + yellow = orange
> yellow + blue = green
> blue + red = purple

If a primary and secondary colour are mixed together (i.e. a mixture of three colours), tertiary colours are created:

> red + green = brown

Complementary colours are colours that lie opposite each other on the colour wheel, for example:

> blue and orange

The three primary colours — red, yellow and blue — create a striking impact, made up in plain cotton fabrics. The design for this block was taken from a collage of torn papers, a section of which was chosen as a repeat pattern. Hand-quilted. (Sue de Barro)

When complementary colours are mixed together they make grey. This is a very important factor to take into account when choosing fabrics. A hanging using, for example, red and green fabrics will appear greyish from a distance and lose much of its attractiveness.

Tones are pure colours mixed with black or white in varying amounts. Tints are colours mixed with whites to give pastel tones. Shades are colours mixed with black.

Analogous colours are those which lie next to each other on the colour circle, for example, yellows, oranges and reds. They usually 'go together' quite well and make satisfying, if somewhat predictable, colour schemes.

Colours are classed as warm or cool — blue is cool, red is warm.

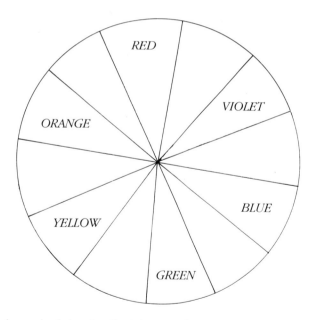

Fig 1 Colour wheel showing the primary colours, red, yellow and blue. When two primaries are mixed together, a secondary colour is formed.

However, a blue can appear warm if placed near red. Warm colours tend to advance, cool colours to recede. These are important factors to consider when designing a quilt, hanging or cushions for a particular room.

The proportion of colour is just as important. A colour scheme consisting of pure colours of equal quantity will often cancel themselves out and appear 'dead'. So also will a colour scheme consisting of equal tonal values. By experimenting with contrasts and differing

(Left) *Strong tonal effects have been achieved by the use of a dark blue and white striped cotton fabric for this striking design based on Folded Star patchwork.* (Diana Mitchell)

(Right) *Folded Star used to create a totally different effect. Plain fabrics have been arranged so that they shade from light at the edge of the work to a darker centre.* (Muriel Fry)

proportions of the colours used, you can eventually achieve an interesting and lively effect.

If your chosen colour scheme is a range of rich, dark colours, try adding a tiny touch of a light, bright colour which will immediately add vitality to your work. If you need a cool, quiet scheme, choose mainly pastel colours but add a small amount of dark colour to give interest.

COLOUR AS A STARTING POINT

A good way to create an interesting colour scheme is to use an existing one, which could be manmade or natural. If you intend to make a quilt for a particular room, why not base your colour scheme on something that is already there? It could be a piece of old china, which will produce a range of beautiful, translucent colours. Or, if you are lucky enough to own one, pick out the colours in a Persian rug which, even if it is old and faded, will produce a range of vibrant tones.

Place your chosen object in a good light and look at the colours very carefully. Make yourself a colour chart by picking out the exact colours you see, using paints, matching threads or fabrics, or a combination of all three. Use the chart to select your fabrics, remembering that it is not necessary to use all the colours in the chart. Colour theory is not particularly easy for the beginner but it is really just a matter of careful observation.

Plain and print silk fabrics show the use of primary and secondary colours in this design for a small cushion in strip patchwork. Hand-quilted with silk thread. (Jenny Bullen)

Colour study based on a tiny, delicate shell. A combination of paint and threads has been used to capture the colours. The patchwork overleaf is worked in colours to match this chart. (Jenny Bullen)

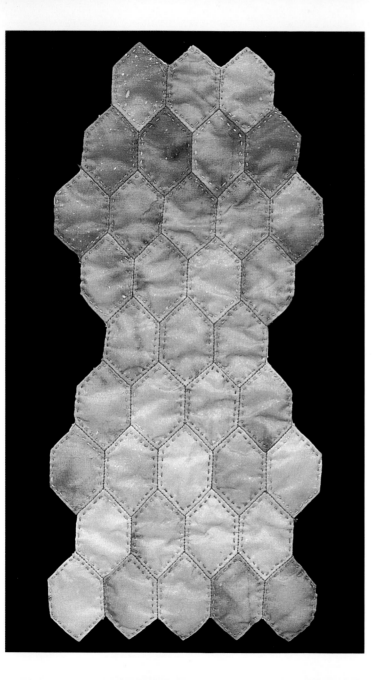

Whenever you embark upon a project, it is very important to allow yourself time to make small experimental pieces, using different colour combinations. This will enable you to select the most pleasing design at an early stage, thus avoiding an expensive disappointment if the finished work does not live up to its promise.

FABRIC PAINTS AND DYES

Painting and dyeing fabric plays an important role in embroidery today and should not be overlooked in patchwork. It is possible to 'customize' fabrics with very little effort. This is great fun to do and requires very little outlay apart from the basic fabric paints or dyes and some fabric.

You will also need cheap sponges, a few brushes, rubber gloves, a plastic bucket for dyes and some mixing plates.

It is advisable to wash all fabrics before you start. Old, well-washed sheeting makes an excellent painting surface and is very useful for experiments.

PERMANENT FABRIC PAINTS

These are readily available in most specialist embroidery shops or craft shops. Because they are painted directly onto the fabric, they are

Fabric paints were used to colour a piece of plain silk fabric. The fabric was then cut up and used in this small hanging of long hexagons. Hand-pieced over paper templates and hand-quilted. (Jenny Bullen)

suitable for use on all types of fabric. They are usually 'fixed' by ironing on the reverse of the design, when dry, with a hot iron. Fabric paints are of quite a thick consistency which makes them suitable for printing on fabric or for painting directly with a brush. They can be thinned by adding water, but this gives them a tendency to spread into the fabric and will also make the colours appear much paler. The colours can be mixed together in various combinations to create other colours (see pages 8–10) so you only really need to buy the three primary colours. It is also possible to buy metallic and pearlized colours in most of the ranges available.

When working with fabric paints, make sure that the work surface is covered in newspaper; the fabric can be taped or pinned to a board if required. Apply the paint to the washed, dry fabric with brushes or a sponge.

The fabric can be sprayed with colour, using either a diffuser (obtained quite cheaply from art shops) or spattering it with an old toothbrush or stencil brush. Aerosol spray guns are available but they are usually quite expensive.

Fabric paints can also be used in conjunction with stencils. Cut a shape out of thin card or oiled stencil board, place it on the fabric, and spray or stipple paint through the hole in the stencil (Fig. 2). It is important to make sure that the fabric is perfectly dry for stencilling or the paint will run.

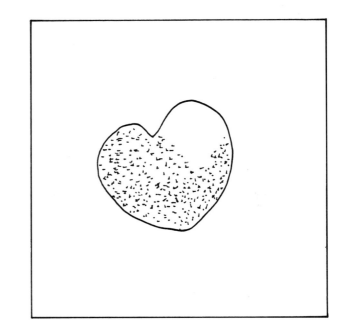

Fig 2 To make a stencil, cut out a shape in thin card or oiled stencil board. Ensure that enough card is left around the motif to protect the surrounding fabric from stray paint.

PRINTING ON FABRIC

Simple printing blocks can be made very easily — one of the simplest and often the most successful is a potato. Slice the potato in half, making sure that the surface is perfectly smooth, and carve out a simple design with a craft knife. Push some undiluted fabric paint onto a household sponge, or roll it out on a smooth surface to use as a pad.

Make sure that the fabric is perfectly dry. It is advisable to tape it to a board. If you wish to use more than one colour, or overprint, wait until the first colour is dry before continuing.

Collect together a variety of simple printing tools — corks, wedges of wood offcuts, sponges, vegetables such as carrots, Brussels sprouts etc. In fact, experiment with anything you think will produce a mark on your fabric (Fig 3). For more intricate designs, or if you wish to print a large area of cloth, lino prints are only slightly more complicated to make.

SILK FABRIC PAINTS

These paints are suitable for use on any type of fabric, although they are particularly good on silk. They are more liquid than permanent fabric paints, and are therefore more suited for painting backgrounds and colour washes than for spraying or printing. There are several different brands available; inspect them with care before buying as some have to be fixed in a steamer or special liquid. Some brands, however, are fixed simply by ironing on the reverse of the fabric.

It is advisable to wash the fabric first, and to tape it to a flat surface. When painting in a background colour, it is easier to start with a dampened fabric as the paint will flow more freely. Paint the fabric with a brush or sponge, allowing the colour to run gently into the background. Use several colours and let them blend into each other to form still more shades. Allow the fabric to dry, then iron it according to the manufacturer's instructions.

If you want to draw with these paints, a thickener called 'gutta' can be purchased. This is used to draw in outlines, and the colours are then painted within the outlined shapes.

Fig 3 A cork makes an ideal printing block. It can be used to build up quite complicated repeat patterns.

(Left) *Cushion in dyed velvets, overprinted in gold. The centre has been further embellished with stitchery.* (Rosie Moore)

TRANSFER PAINTS

These paints are quite different to the two other types already mentioned in that they are painted on paper, and then ironed onto the fabric when dry. They are intended primarily for manmade fabrics but work very well on poly/cotton blends. It is now possible to buy a solution which allows them to be used on cottons as well.

The important point to remember when using these paints is that the colour on the paper will often not be the same when ironed onto the fabric. Colours react differently on different types of fabric, so it is important to experiment first. Remember, too, that a reverse, or mirror image will appear on the fabric; this is an important point to be borne in mind when using lettering, for instance.

Any of the painting and printing methods that I have described can be used in conjunction with transfer paints but they must all be applied to paper first. The ideal paper to use should be non-absorbent, such as top-quality typing paper.

When the paint has dried on the paper, place it carefully over the fabric and pin in place. Heat the iron to the correct temperature (instructions are given on the paint bottles) and iron over the fabric, taking care not to leave the iron in one place for too long. The same design can be used again, but each time the image will appear paler.

Certain types of paper bags and wrapping papers can also be ironed onto manmade fabrics. They are frequently used by florists to wrap flowers and are usually quite thin with a slightly shiny surface. The paper should be placed face down on the fabric and pressed with a hot iron. As with the transfer paints, the finished result is somewhat unpredictable.

Strips of assorted synthetic fabrics were machined together to form a ground fabric. Transfer paints were used to print paper which, when dry, was cut into strips, laid across the background fabric and ironed. The paper was then removed, leaving the colour on the fabric. The piece was hand-quilted. (Jenny Bullen)

Transfer crayons can be purchased very cheaply and are great fun to try. They are used in the same way as ordinary children's crayons, first on paper and then ironed onto the fabric.

DYE BATHS

Very exciting results can be obtained with patchwork if a variety of different types of fabric are all placed together in the same dye bath. The simplest method is to use cold water reactive dyes, which are easily obtainable in small quantities and are not very expensive. You will also need a bucket and a pair of rubber gloves. It is always advisable to wear a protective mask when using powder dyes of any kind, and these can be bought quite cheaply at DIY stores.

Collect together an assortment of fabrics in natural fibres, including plain and printed fabrics, which can be very interesting when over-dyed. Remember that dark colours cannot be dyed to lighter shades.

It is important to follow the manufacturer's instructions. You may also find the following information useful:

1 Weigh the fabrics before dyeing and use the correct amount of dye for the weight.
2 Wash all fabrics first to remove any dressing.
3 Use a vessel large enough to contain enough water to cover the fabrics and allow for manipulation.
4 Rinse the fabric thoroughly after dyeing.

It is now possible to buy dyes especially for use in automatic washing machines. They work very well, although they are more expensive.

An assortment of natural fabrics, including silks and plain and printed cottons, were all placed together in the same dye bath. The pieces were then sewn together in the form of strip patchwork. Hand-quilted. (Jenny Bullen)

DYEING WITH TEA

This is a very simple method of dyeing, used to give an 'antique' look to fabrics and to tone down bright or garish colours.

Method

1 Collect together an assortment of fabrics; pure cottons work best. Wash and leave them to soak before using.
2 Place five or six teabags in a large saucepan of cold water and bring to the boil. Boil for about ten minutes and remove the teabags.
3 Place the fabric in the saucepan and bring the water back to the boil for approximately 15 minutes, stirring the fabric frequently.
4 Add half a cup of white vinegar to the water and boil for a further ten minutes.
5 Remove the fabric from the saucepan and rinse thoroughly. Dry away from direct heat.

Deeper tones can be achieved by using more teabags.

A small quilt in various fabrics, including synthetics, based on the Windmill block. After it was made up, the whole top was put in a pink dye bath. Hand-quilted. (Valerie McCallum)

(Right) *Detail of 'Flotilla', a wall hanging worked in the Log Cabin method, using a triangular instead of a square block. All the fabrics were hand-dyed.* (Muriel Fry. In the collection of Lord Walpole)

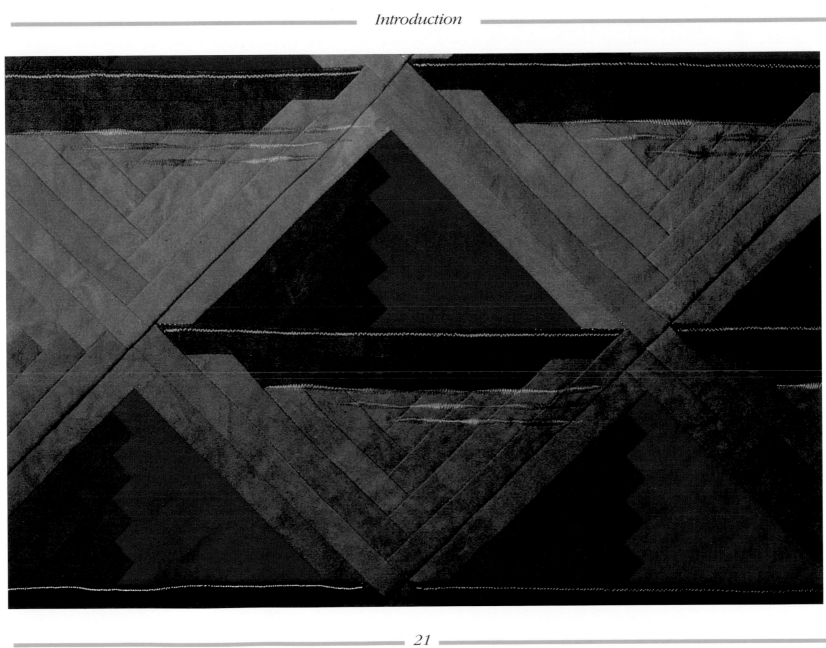

DYEING IN A MICROWAVE OVEN

If you have a microwave oven, you can achieve tie-dyed or space-dyed effects using cold water reactive dyes.

You will need dye powder, a bowl suitable for use in the microwave, a plastic bag, plastic spoon and rubber gloves.

Method

1 Wash the fabric before use. It can be used wet or dried, depending on the required effects. Different effects can be achieved by knotting, pleating or folding the fabric, or simply rolling it into a ball.
2 Place the dye in the bowl and gradually add $\frac{1}{2}$ pint of water. Stir thoroughly to dissolve the dye. Add another $\frac{1}{2}$ pint of water.
3 Place the fabric in the bowl and work the dye into the fabric.
4 Cover the bowl with the plastic bag.
5 Put the bowl into the microwave and set on 'High' for four minutes.
6 After four minutes, remove the bowl from the oven. Remember to protect your hands from the heat.
7 Tip away the dye solution and rinse the fabric in cold water. To protect the pattern, do not undo any knots, pleats, etc. until the first of the dye has been rinsed away.
8 When the water is running almost clear, wash the fabric in hot water with your normal washing powder to remove any remaining dye.
9 Dry the fabric away from direct heat and sunlight.

An irregular Log Cabin block, using fabrics dyed in a microwave. (Margaret Rivers)

2

HAND-SEWN TECHNIQUES

Hand-sewn patchwork is very time-consuming, something which should be taken into account if you are about to embark on a quilt for a double bed. Other, quicker methods are described in Chapter 3. However, hand-piecing is a very attractive technique and I firmly believe that this method still has a place in the present-day craft. One of its attractions is that it takes up very little space and can therefore be worked on away from home.

As well as the techniques described in this section, hand-sewn patchwork is also covered in Chapter 3, where instructions for hand sewing each design follow the machine sewing instructions.

EQUIPMENT

Only very basic equipment is required for the hand-sewn techniques:

scissors — a good-quality pair for cutting fabric, and another pair for cutting paper and card
needles — these should be quite fine ('betweens', these days often called 'quilting', are particularly good)
fine pins
thimble
beeswax is useful to wax sewing threads to strengthen them and prevent tangles

You will also need one or two purchased metal templates, some old greetings cards, a ruler and a pencil.

MOSAIC PATCHWORK

Mosaic patchwork is made up of single patches — hexagons, diamonds, triangles, etc. — sewn together to make a whole. The patches consist of fabric carefully turned and tacked over paper, and then sewn together by hand.

This method seems to be a very traditional English form of patchwork and appears to have gathered momentum towards the end of the eighteenth century. At first it would only have been worked by women in the upper classes of society because paper was still quite a scarce commodity and leisure time was unknown among the lower classes.

During the Victorian period, the craft was taken up with great enthusiasm by the emerging middle classes. Old letters and documents were often cut up and used for the paper patches. Many examples survive from this period unfinished, with the papers still tacked in place, and one can only assume that patchwork was a kind of therapy for bored housewives! These women had servants to cook and clean for them, and presumably enough woven blankets for their beds as the completed tops were very rarely quilted.

Materials

You will need a master template, preferably metal, obtainable at specialist shops (see page 93). It is possible to make your own from thin, stiff card but they must be accurately cut (Fig 4 on p. 28). You will also need thin card or good-quality paper for the patches, your usual sewing equipment (see left), fabrics, tacking thread and pure

A panel showing a variety of different types of patchwork, including strip patchwork, Folded Star, Cathedral Window, woven strips, blocks, mosaic patchwork and Clamshell. The fabrics used are plain and hand-dyed cottons and silks. (Linda Cook)

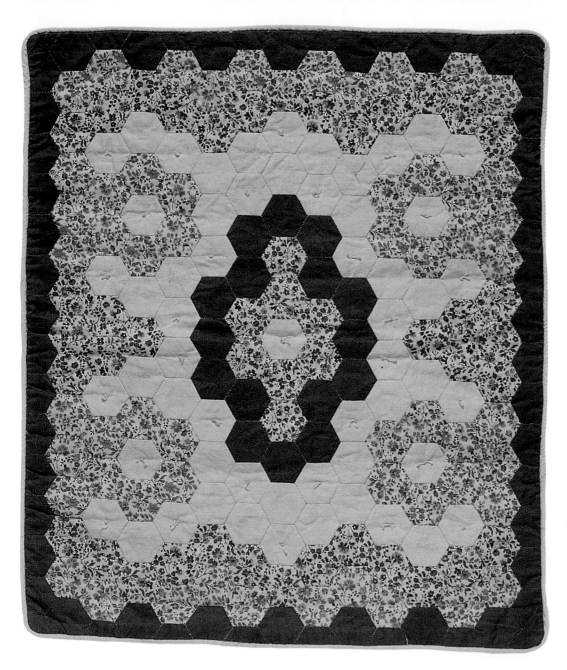

(Left) *A small mosaic cot quilt in hexagons, using plain and printed cottons. Tie-quilted.* (Jenny Bullen)

(Right) *An unfinished Victorian mosaic patchwork made of hexagons, with the papers still in place. An assortment of mostly plain fabrics, including silks, satins and rayons.*

cotton sewing threads to match the colours of the fabrics you are using.

The variety of fabrics available has already been mentioned and most of them are suitable for mosaic patchwork. However, if this is your first attempt, pure dressweight cotton is probably the most suitable as it will crease beautifully. Polyester cotton mixes are crease-resistant and therefore more difficult to handle.

Method of working

1 To cut out the paper patches, hold the metal template firmly against the paper and cut out a patch, with the blades of the scissors touching the template. Do not use your best dressmaking scissors to cut paper as it will soon blunt them.
2 To make the fabric patches, lay the fabric on a flat surface, having

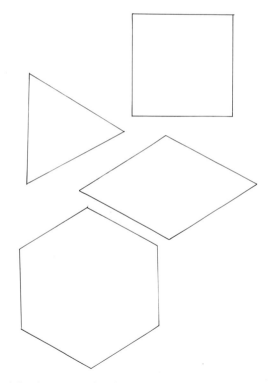

Fig 4 *Some of the shapes suitable for mosaic patchwork: square, triangle, diamond and hexagon.*

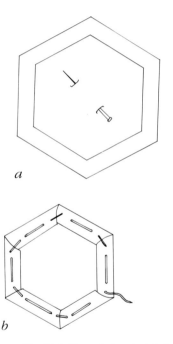

a

b

Fig 5(a) *Pin a paper patch to the fabric, ensuring that one edge of the patch lies on the straight grain of the fabric. Cut out, leaving a 6 mm ($\frac{1}{4}$ in) seam allowance.*
(b) *Press the seam allowances firmly over the paper patch and tack in place.*

first carefully ironed out any creases. Pin a paper patch on the straight grain of the fabric and carefully cut out, leaving a 6 mm ($\frac{1}{4}$ in) seam allowance all round (Fig 5a).

3 Finger-press the seam allowance firmly over the paper patch and tack in place (Fig 5b): It is especially important to ensure that the corners are carefully sewn down. If you are confident enough, it is not necessary to start with a knot in the thread or to work a back stitch to finish, as this will speed up the process of removing the papers later.

4 When several patches are tacked in place, they can be sewn together. It is a good idea to place all the shapes on a cork mat or a piece of polystyrene so that you can see the design. Use a sewing thread to match the colour of the fabric; it helps to run the thread through a piece of beeswax to prevent the thread from knotting or fraying. Place two patches right sides together and sew with tiny oversewn stitches, making sure that you do not catch the paper in the stitching (Fig 6a).

5 When the piece of patchwork has been completed, the paper patches can be removed (Fig 6b). Carefully snip the tacking threads. Pull out the papers and any remaining tacking threads. Press the work on the wrong side with a steam iron, under a damp cloth; make sure that all the seams lie flat. Do not iron the work until all the tacking threads and papers have been removed or you may find that you have permanently ironed the stitch indentations into the fabric!

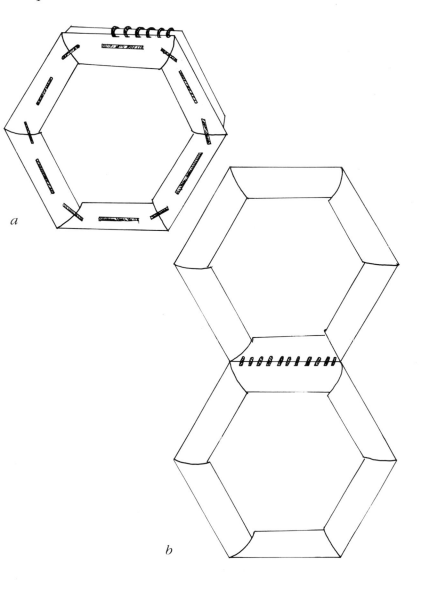

Fig 6(a) To join the patches, place them right sides together and oversew, being careful not to catch the paper patches in the stitching.
(b) When all the patches have been sewn together, remove the tacking threads and pull out the paper patches.

Design suggestions

'Hexagons are so boring!' is the cry one often hears today. And so they will be if the same 'safe' colours and print fabrics are used over and over again. It is possible to produce exciting, original work if you consider the surface of the patchwork as a whole.

Mosaic patchwork is very suitable for difficult fabrics — velvet and other pile fabrics, slippery silks, etc. You can use these fabrics to produce a rich, textured surface which can be further embellished with surface stitchery, beads, sequins and gold thread. Care must be taken when working with pile fabrics; do not leave pins or tacking threads in the fabric for too long or it may be impossible to remove the marks. If you intend to make something, such as a small purse, where extra stiffening will be needed, Vilene can be used instead of paper for the patches; instead of taking the tacking threads through to the surface, use herringbone stitch to attach the fabric to the Vilene patches.

Use fabric paints to create an interesting surface. Sponge colours onto dampened fabric (try silk, or polyester cotton which has a slight sheen to it). When the fabric has dried and been ironed to set it, cut it into patches and arrange them to form a pleasing design.

The reverse of the patchwork could be an exciting base for experimental work. The Victorians used love letters for their patches. Why not copy this idea? Alternatively, handmade paper or dyed or coloured paper patches could be used and left in the work. The edges of the fabric turnings could be frayed out. The tacking stitches could be left in and made more decorative, and other stitchery added to the work.

A quilt depicting the church and some of the houses in the famous cricketing village of Hambledon in Hampshire. The entire project was hand-stitched over papers and hand-quilted. (Cynthia Sherwood)

Detail, showing the church. (Cynthia Sherwood)

Use shapes other than hexagons, or combine different shapes in one piece of work. The pattern known as Tumbling Blocks (often called Baby Blocks) is created with a diamond template to produce complex three-dimensional results. You must take great care to separate your fabrics into groups of light, medium and dark tones. Use isometric paper to work out the designs (Fig 7, overleaf), and coloured pencils to block in shapes. If you are clever enough, it is possible to create an undulating surface, three-dimensional in some places and a flat plane in others.

(Left) *The reverse of an unfinished piece of Victorian patchwork with the papers still in place.*

(Right) *Tumbling Blocks, or Baby Blocks, showing a dramatic three-dimensional effect. Worked in cotton fabrics.* (Jenny Bullen)

Fig 7 Isometric paper can be used to work out designs for mosaic patchwork. Block in the shapes with coloured pencils.

An unfinished Victorian quilt, worked in the Tumbling Blocks design. Mostly rayon fabrics.

FOLDED PATCHWORK

This technique includes designs such as Cathedral Window and Folded Star, in which squares of fabric are folded and sewn together to form a surface. It is not as time-consuming as mosaic patchwork but care must be taken when cutting and manipulating the fabric.

FOLDED STAR

Often called Somerset Patchwork, squares of fabric are folded into triangles and arranged to form a pleasing design.

Materials

Use fabrics that will crease easily. Fine cottons are ideal, of course. This design works well if shades of dark and light fabrics are used. A square of backing fabric, such as calico, will also be needed, as well as the usual sewing equipment (see page 24).

Method of working

1 Cut out squares of fabric — 5 cm (2 in) square is a good size (Fig 8a). It is quite useful to make a master template, especially if you are cutting out a large number of squares.
2 Fold the fabric in half, with the wrong side of the fabric together (Fig 8b).
3 Fold over and press the points on the folded edge to the centre so that they meet at the raw edges and form a triangle (Fig 8c).

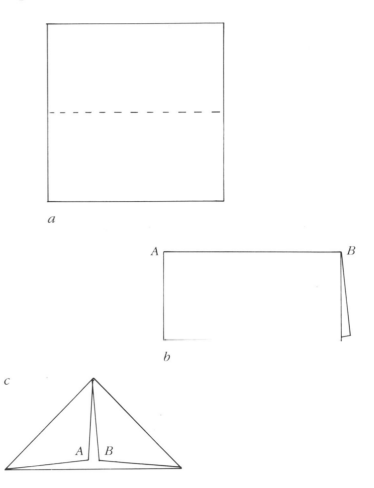

(Left) *Folded Star patchwork worked in a traditional circular design. Plain and printed cottons.* (Jenny Bullen)

Fig 8(a) Cut out squares of fabric, all of the same size.
(b) Fold the squares in half, with the wrong side of the fabric inside.

(c) Fold over and press points A and B so that they meet at the raw edges and produce a triangular shape.

4 Mark the centre point on the backing fabric and pin the first four patches in place, with the points meeting in the centre (Fig 9a). Oversew the points together and sew down the raw edges, using running stitches (Fig 9b).

5 For the next row, eight patches will be needed. Pin them in place with the points approximately 1 cm ($\frac{3}{8}$ in) from the centre point and the edges overlapping. Sew carefully in place. Continue in this way, adding more patches to each row until the desired size has been reached.

Folded Star patchwork can be used as an edging to decorate cushions, wall hangings, etc. (Fig 10).

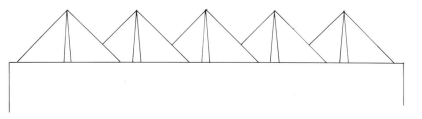

Fig 10 Folded Star patchwork can be used as a decorative edging.

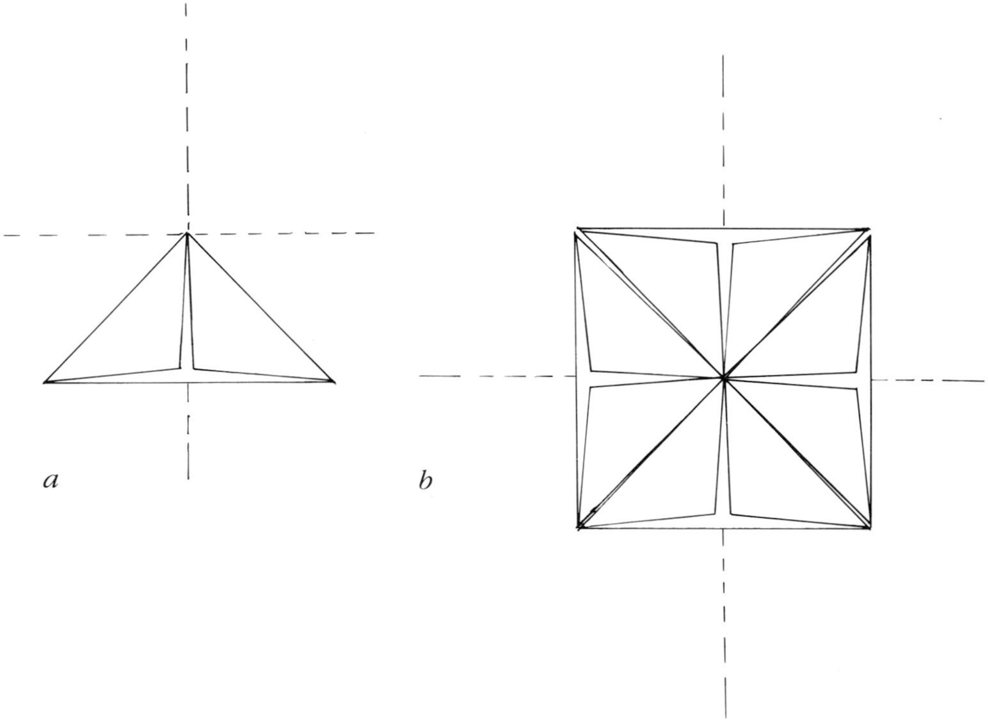

a

b

Fig 9(a) Mark the centre point on the backing fabric and pin the first patch in place, with the point placed on the centre point of the fabric. (b) Pin the other three patches in place. Oversew the points and sew down the raw edges.

*Folded Star patches laid in overlapping rows.
Silks and lurex fabrics. Decorated with hand
embroidery, using metallic machine embroidery
threads, and small tassels in fine silk thread.
(Jenny Bullen)*

Design suggestions

Colour and tone are important points to remember in the Folded Star technique. Different shades of one colour are effective, possibly with the darkest shade in the centre. Thick fabrics will not work particularly well, but it is worth trying silks, shot fabrics, stripes and lurex. Instead of placing the patches so that the points all meet in the centre, arrange them in overlapping rows. Sew a bead or a tiny glittery tassel to some of the points. Experiment with patches of different sizes in the same piece of work.

Cushion based on Folded Star patchwork. Dyed and printed fabrics, embellished with machine embroidery and handmade cords and tassels. (Rosie Moore)

CATHEDRAL WINDOW

This folded patchwork technique is ideal for experimenting with unusual fabrics. However, it does depend on careful and accurate cutting and sewing, or the finished appearance will not be good.

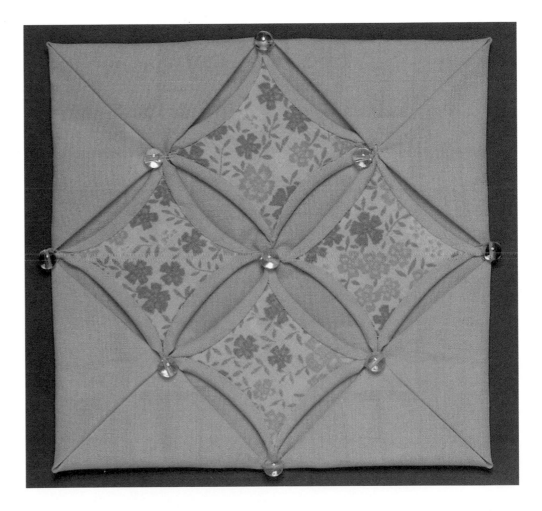

Small sample of Cathedral Window patchwork. Plain and printed cottons, decorated with beads. (Sue de Barro)

Materials

The background fabric is traditionally calico but any good-quality fabric is suitable. If you use calico, do make sure that it is of a fine quality and that it is not creased.

The centres of the 'windows' are usually in a contrasting colour to the background fabric and are often patterned. Any fabric can be used, including lurex, velvets, silks, etc.

Method of working

1 Using the background fabric, cut out a number of squares, all of the same size — 14–18 cm (6–7 in) is a good size. They must all be cut very accurately.

2 Turn under 6 mm (¼ in) turnings and press (Fig 11a).
3 Fold the four corners into the centre and pin in place (Fig 11b).
4 Repeat step 3. Using a matching thread and tiny stitches, secure the corners in the centre of the square.
5 Make other squares in the same way and join them all together with small oversewn stitches (Fig 11c). When two squares are sewn together, a diamond shape is formed.
6 For the centre patches, cut out several small squares in contrasting fabric (Fig 12a). They should be 6 mm (¼ in) smaller than the diamond shape formed by the backing fabrics.
7 Pin the squares in place. Turn the edges of the backing fabric over the raw edges and hem in place (Fig 12b).

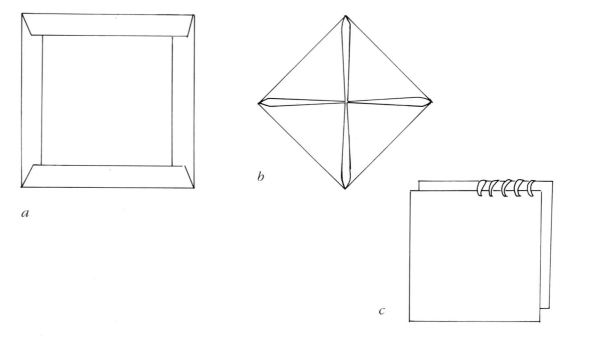

Fig 11(a) Cut out squares of backing fabric, all of the same size. It is important to ensure that they are all cut as accurately as possible. Turn under and press a bare 6 mm (¼ in) turning on each side.
(b) Fold the four corners into the centre. Repeat, then pin the corners in place.
(c) To join the squares together, place them right sides together and oversew with tiny stitches.

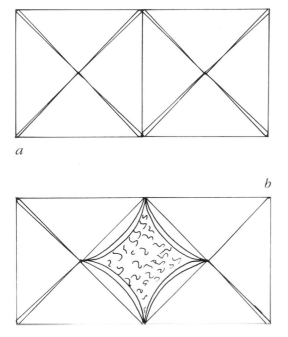

a

b

Fig 12(a) For the centre patches, cut squares of contrasting fabric, slightly smaller than the diamond shape formed by the backing fabrics. (b) Pin the squares in place. Roll the edges of the backing fabric over the raw edges and hem in place.

'Susie's Sampler.' A bed quilt, machine pieced and hand and machine quilted, using cotton fabrics and polyester cotton wadding. The quilt has a piped edging. The design evolved from Katie Pasquini's book, The Contemporary Sampler. (Ann Ohlenschlager)

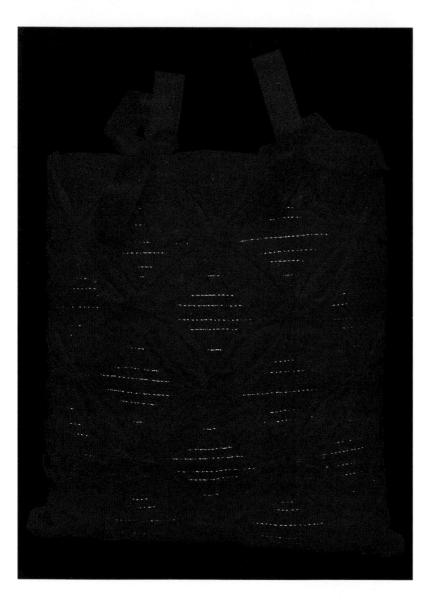

Design suggestions

The backing fabric is usually plain and the centre patterned. Try working the other way around. Experiment with striped fabrics — use the same fabric for the centre squares but arrange it so that the stripes form interesting patterns.

Make the centre squares in rich brocade or lurex, and the backing fabric very dark, to give a rich, jewelled effect. Embellish the squares with beads or sequins.

The centre squares could all be embroidered, but beware of trying to embroider different scenes in each square as the result looks somewhat fragmented. A piece of machine-embroidered fabric could be cut up and used.

Experiment with transparent fabrics. What will happen to all the seams? Could they be incorporated into the design? Decorative papers are another possibility.

(Left) *Tiny cushion in Cathedral Window patchwork, worked in red silk with red silk insets and decorated with rows of machine stitchery in lurex threads.* (Christine Cooper)

(Right) *An interesting use of Cathedral Window patchwork, with fabric tucked inside the backing fabric and the diamond insets left plain. Hand-dyed cotton and velvet. The pink fabric is decorated with embroidery, and tiny Suffolk Puffs (see page 52) have been added.* (Pam Scott)

APPLIED PATCHWORK

This includes techniques such as crazy patchwork and Clamshell, where patches are applied, or sewn down on to, a backing fabric.

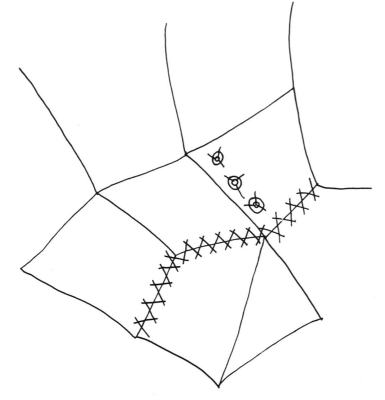

Fig 13 In crazy patchwork, scraps of exotic fabrics are sewn down on to a backing fabric with decorative embroidery stitches. It is often embellished with beads and sequins.

CRAZY PATCHWORK

This was very much a Victorian invention. Scraps of exotic fabrics, such as velvets, silks or satins, were sewn down in a seemingly random way, held together with decorative embroidery stitches and embellished with beads or sequins (Figs 13 and 14).

Experiment with fabrics and different embroidery stitches, but remember that it is not easy to achieve an apparently totally random effect. It would be interesting to collect together a range of different types of fabric in one colour, perhaps white or neutrals, and sew them in place with a self-coloured thread.

To prevent the fabric from fraying, use Bondaweb to apply the patches to the fabric. This is a double-sided adhesive sheet to which fabric is applied, using a hot iron. The backing paper is then peeled away and the fabric can be applied to a second piece of fabric.

Crazy patchwork is not a particularly practical method of patchwork but it is fun and worth trying.

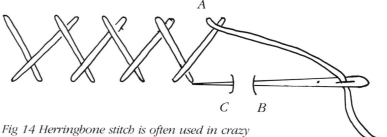

Fig 14 Herringbone stitch is often used in crazy patchwork. Bring the needle out of the fabric at A on the upper line. Insert the needle at B on the lower line and bring it out again at C, then insert it again on the upper line.

(Right) *Silk fabrics were used in this crazy patchwork sample, with hand embroidery, beads and tiny sequins.* (Jenny Bullen)

Crazy patchwork in assorted fabrics decorated with surface embroidery, using stitches found on Victorian crazy patchwork. (Diana Mitchell)

CLAMSHELL

Materials

Clamshell is a very attractive design but quite time-consuming. Cottons and cotton blends are probably the most suitable fabrics to use. Heavier-weight fabrics will not be easy to work with. You will need a backing fabric such as calico, matching sewing cotton and the usual sewing equipment (see page 24).

Method of working

1 Make a card template or use a purchased metal one. Cut out a number of fabric shapes, with a 6 mm ($\frac{1}{4}$ in) seam allowance around the curved edge only (Fig 15a). (The lower edges will be hidden when the patchwork is joined together.)

2 Turn under and tack the seam allowance on the curved edge (Fig 15b).

3 When all the patches have been prepared in this way, arrange them on a backing fabric so that they overlap and all the raw edges are covered (Fig 16).

4 Pin the patches in place. When you are satisfied with the result, hem the patches to the backing fabric. Remove all the tacking threads and carefully press the finished piece.

a   b

Fig 15(a) Make a card template, or use a purchased metal one. Using this template as a guide, cut out a number of fabric shapes, with a 6 mm ($\frac{1}{4}$ in) seam allowance round the curved edge only. (b) Turn under the seam allowance on the curved edge and tack in place.

Fig 16 Arrange the patches on the backing fabric and pin in place, so that the lower edges of each patch are covered by the row below.

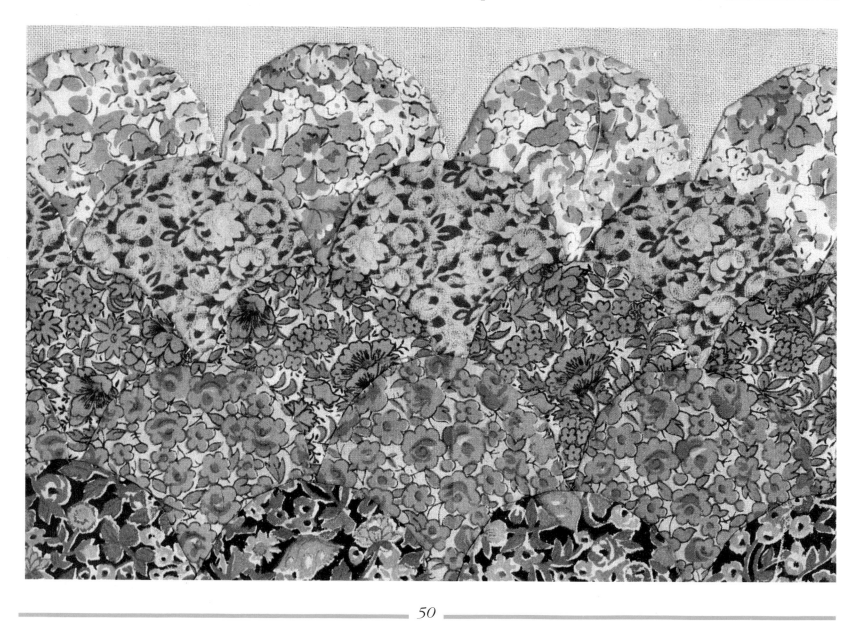

Design suggestions

Clamshell makes quite a robust fabric, so it would be suitable for cushions, cot quilts and even simple garments.

Very pleasing designs can be made by shading the colours from light to dark across the surface of the fabric. Try working with a variety of fabrics, such as lurex, hand-dyed fabrics, etc. Add surface decoration in the form of hand embroidery, beads, sequins or narrow ribbons.

An alternative method for machine patchwork is to cut out all the fabrics without any seam allowance and apply them to the backing fabric using Bondaweb (see page 46). Hold them in place with a machine satin stitch, or several rows of free machining. Using this method, experiment with different-size patches in one design.

(Left) *Clamshell patchwork, using Liberty Tana lawn fabrics on a calico ground.* (Jenny Bullen)

(Right) *Detail of the photograph on page 25, showing Suffolk Puffs, Tumbling Blocks and Clamshells on a strip patchwork ground.* (Linda Cook)

OTHER HAND-SEWN TECHNIQUES

Patchwork is often thought of as a flat surface but there are several techniques which you can use to make your work three-dimensional. We have already seen what can be achieved with Cathedral Window, a form of folded patchwork; another quite different technique is Suffolk Puffs.

SUFFOLK PUFFS

This is a hand-sewn technique in which circles, or 'puffs', of gathered fabric are joined together to make a whole.

Materials

Any fabric would be suitable, although heavier-weight fabrics will be very difficult to handle. Fabrics that fray easily should be avoided.

Method of working

1 You will need a circular template, cut out of thin card. Any circular object, such as a saucer, small tin, etc. could also be used.
2 Lay the fabric on a flat surface and draw round the template. Carefully cut out each patch.
3 On the wrong side of the fabric, turn under a narrow hem and press. Using a matching sewing thread, secure the hem with small running stitches (Fig 17a). Pull up the thread tightly so that each patch is doubled over, then fasten off (Fig 17b).
4 Arrange the circles in a design. Join them together with tiny oversewn stitches just at the points where they touch (Fig 18).

Design suggestions

Suffolk Puffs are rather an impractical method of patchwork, although they could be used for cot quilts or small wall hangings.

It is, however, a good technique for experimental work. Try using different-size circles in the same piece of work. Use hand-coloured fabrics or fabrics dyed in a toning range of colours. Add embroidery in the form of hand stitchery, decorative beads, tassels or ribbons. The centre of each patch could also be filled with interesting fabrics.

Small pieces of wadding could be used to give added warmth. Experiment with transfer dyes on synthetic wadding to match or contrast with the fabrics used.

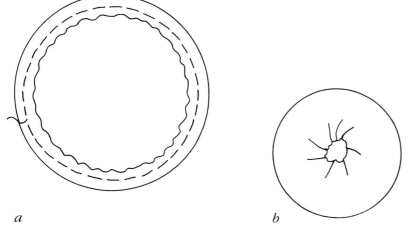

a   *b*

Fig 17(a) Cut out each fabric shape. On the wrong side, turn under a narrow hem and sew in place with small running stitches. Do not fasten off. (b) Pull up the sewing thread so that the patch is doubled over and fasten securely.

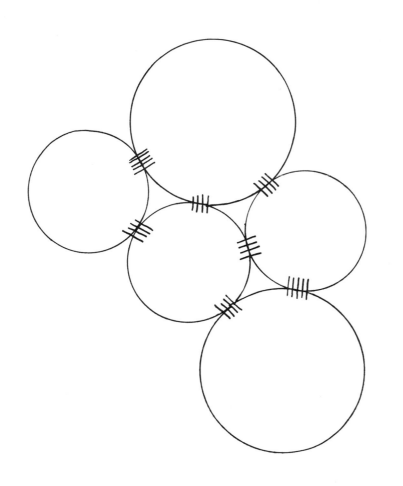

Fig 18 Stitch the circles together just at the points where each patch touches the next.

(Right) *Suffolk Puffs in silk organza, hand-dyed to match the colours of a shell (see page 13). Decorated with a small amount of hand stitchery in metallic thread.* (Jenny Bullen)

MACHINE-SEWN TECHNIQUES

USING a sewing machine to make patchwork considerably speeds up the process. It is not at all difficult to do as long as the fabric patches are carefully and accurately cut. Any straight stitch machine will do, even one without an electric motor, as long as it is cleaned and oiled regularly.

The requirements are the same as for hand sewing, with the addition of graph paper and strong card for making templates, sewing machine thread, and of course, a sewing machine.

Most of the techniques described in this section can also be worked by hand, and instructions are given for both methods. However, the machine-sewing method is infinitely quicker and should not be despised by those who favour hand-sewn patchwork.

LOG CABIN

This is one of the most popular of all patchwork techniques. It is associated with the early settlers in North America, who lived in rough-hewn log cabins. The square in the centre of each block was traditionally red or orange, to represent the firelight in the centre of the cabin. The surrounding oblong patches represent the log walls, half in light and half in shadow.

Log Cabin is very attractive and economical, and the temptation is to use up scraps of whatever fabric is to hand. This is, of course, perfectly acceptable but for the finished design to work effectively the fabrics must be sorted into two distinct collections — either two

colours, such as blue and green, or dark and light tones of the same colour.

Method of working

1 Sort the fabrics and choose a colour for the centre square; this is usually plain but need not be so. It should, however, form a definite contrast to the strips that will surround it. The size of the square can range from 2–5 cm (1–2 in). When cutting out, remember to include a seam allowance of 6 mm ($\frac{1}{4}$ in) on each edge. A square that is to have a finished size of 4 cm ($1\frac{1}{2}$ in), for example, will need to be cut out at 5 cm (2 in). If you are cutting out several squares, it is advisable to make an accurate card template. There is no need to mark the seam allowances on the fabric.

2 Prepare the fabric strips, first by sorting them into two piles, one of each colour or one dark and one light. The width of the strip is entirely personal but the strips must all be the same width throughout the block, and therefore the quilt (unless you are experimenting). A finished width of 2–2.5 cm ($\frac{3}{4}$–1 in) is probably sufficient, but remember to include seam allowances of 6 mm ($\frac{1}{4}$ in) on each edge. Cut the strips the entire width of the fabric but do not be tempted to tear the cloth, as this will result in a much narrower strip with frayed edges. To cut out, press each fabric piece, fold in half and, if possible, in half again. Use a ruler to mark the strips on the fabric, then cut carefully along the marked lines.

3 Thread the sewing machine with a matching coloured thread.

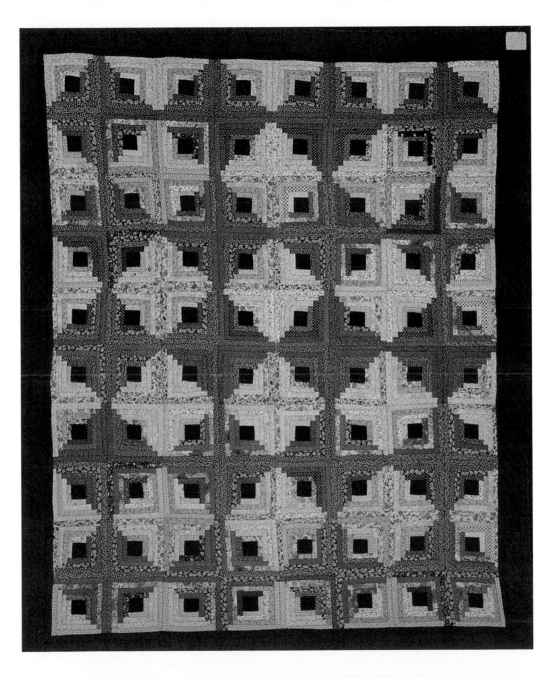

Log Cabin quilt in assorted cotton fabrics with plain red centres, arranged in the traditional Sunshine and Shadow design. Machine-pieced and hand-quilted. (Jenny Bullen)

4 Pin the first strip right side down to the centre patch, with the raw edges together (Fig 19a). Cut the strip to the same length as the centre square.

5 Place the fabric under the sewing machine foot and line up the raw edges of the fabric with the outside edge of the foot. Machine along the edge of the strip. Do not back stitch at either end but cut off the thread, leaving a short length of cotton. This will make any unpicking easier, and the thread ends will be secured by subsequent lengths of stitching.

6 Press the seam with the seam allowances together, away from the centre patch (Fig 19b).

7 Turn the patch clockwise. Pin and stitch the next strip in place (Fig 19c). Press each seam in turn.

8 On the third side, repeat the process but this time with a strip of fabric from the second pile of colours.

9 Repeat for the fourth side (Fig 19d). Continue building up the strips until the block is the required size, remembering to keep the two sets of colours distinct.

10 Make more blocks in the same way.

11 Press each block and check that they all are of the same size. Arrange them on a flat surface. Pin and then machine each block together to form rows. Pin the rows together very carefully, matching all seams, then stitch.

Sewing by hand

Method 1

The blocks are prepared and joined together in the method described above, except that they are all sewn by hand.

Pin the first strip right side down to the centre patch, with the raw edges together, and cut away the excess strip. Use a matching thread and begin with a knot. Join the seam with small running stitches, finishing off with two or three stitches worked on top of each other. Continue as described for machine sewing.

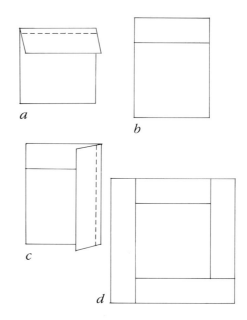

Fig 19(a) Pin the first strip to the centre patch and stitch in place.
(b) Press the seam allowances together, away from the centre square.
(c) Turn the fabric clockwise and sew the second strip in place.
(d) Repeat for the third and fourth sides of the square, pressing each seam in turn.

Method 2
This involves sewing all the strips to a fabric background. It is particularly useful if you are working with difficult fabrics that might slip or fray. Either hand or machine sewing can be used.

1 Cut a square of backing fabric, such as calico, and mark on it the diagonals.
2 Pin the centre square to the centre of the backing square and tack in place.
3 Pin the first strip right side down against one edge of the centre square and sew through all layers of fabric. Turn to the right side and press in place. Continue until all the strips have been sewn in place (Fig 20).

This method is not often used when the finished patchwork is to be quilted as the extra backing fabric would make the work heavy and rather difficult to hand-quilt. It would be very suitable, however, for wall hangings or other projects where a flatter effect is required.

Log Cabin cushion in Liberty Tana lawn fabrics. Machine-pieced and hand-quilted. (Jenny Bullen)

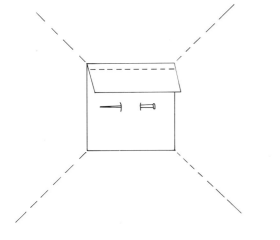

Fig 20 Place the centre square on the backing fabric and tack in place. Pin the first strip to the square, with right sides together, and stitch through all the layers of fabric. Press in place. Continue in this way until the block is the required size.

Design suggestions

Log Cabin blocks were traditionally arranged in various patterns, including Straight Furrow, Barn Raising, Streak o' Lightning etc., and these are still very effective (Fig 21). Courthouse Steps is another variation, in which strips of the same colour are placed on opposite, not adjoining, sides (Fig 22). However, Log Cabin is also a method that lends itself to modern experimentation, remembering, of course, the aims of the project and the suitability of the fabrics.

The centre square could be made much more interesting with the addition of embroidery, or fabric that has been tucked or pleated. It could be made of two or more different fabrics, or printed with a simple potato or lino block.

Use triangles instead of a square. Experiment with triangles of different shapes, which will result in a variety of different-shaped blocks. This may give rise to some difficulties when you come to sewing the blocks together, but these can be overcome with careful planning. To sew strips to triangular centres, allow enough extra fabric at each end so that they are covered by the next set of strips.

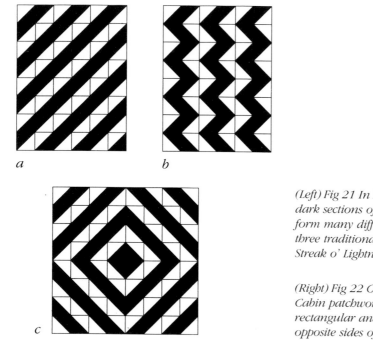

a

b

c

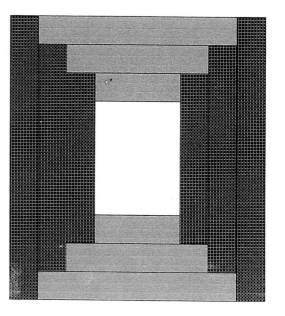

(Left) Fig 21 In Log Cabin patchwork, the light and dark sections of each block can be arranged to form many different designs. Illustrated here are three traditional patterns: (a) Straight Furrow, (b) Streak o' Lightning, (c) Barn Raising.

(Right) Fig 22 Courthouse Steps, a variation of Log Cabin patchwork. The centre patch is often rectangular and the contrasting patches are set at opposite sides of the patch.

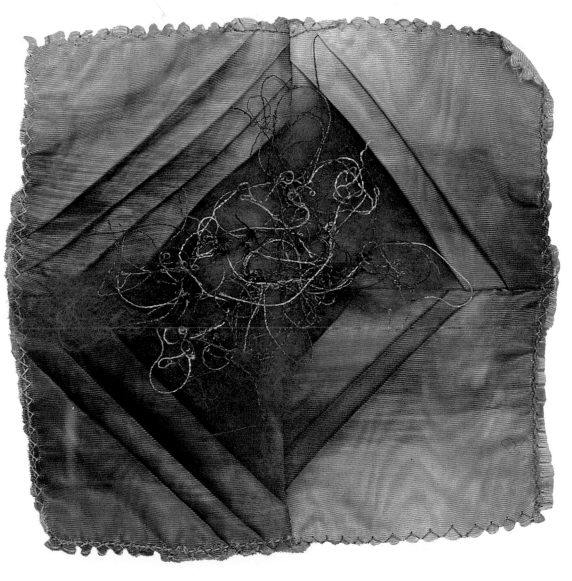

Irregular Log Cabin block. Random fabric around a centre square of machine-embroidered fabric. (Sue de Barro)

(Left) *'How Does Your Garden Grow?' Wall hanging in hand-dyed fabrics. Folded Star patches form the centres of the blocks, surrounded by Log Cabin patchwork.* (Muriel Fry)

(Below) *Log Cabin patchwork block in hand-dyed fabrics, incorporating textured threads and Folded Star patches.* (Diana Mitchell)

(Right) *Log Cabin patchwork used to depict a landscape which shows an actual log cabin.* (Maureen Thomas)

(Far right) *'Eastern Lights'. Panel using Log Cabin patchwork as a design source. Dyed and printed decorative papers sewn around centre squares of lurex fabric.* (Jenny Bullen)

The strips can be of exotic fabrics, such as velvet, silk or lurex. Experiment with decorative papers, hand-dyed or printed, and transparent fabrics.

Cut the strips in different widths; this needs some careful planning but leads to very interesting results. Finally, the centre square does not have to be placed in the centre. It could be offset, with strips sewn to two sides only.

SEMINOLE PATCHWORK

This type of patchwork is worked solely by machine as it relies on strips of fabric sewn together. These strips are then cut up and rearranged to form new designs, which would make it impossible to sew by hand.

Seminole patchwork is named after the tribes of American Indians who were resettled in the Florida swamplands. In the late nineteenth century they were given sewing machines and developed their own unique method of working. There are many variations in design, some of which are extremely complicated and involve the use of very narrow strips of fabric. When each strip of patchwork has been worked, they are sewn together with bands of fabric of varying widths to create the finished design.

Method of working

Collect together a variety of cotton fabrics. Traditionally, plain colours were used for Seminole patchwork, but it is equally possible to use patterned fabrics.

1 Using the full width of the fabric, carefully cut out the strips to the required size.
2 With right sides together, place two strips under the foot of the sewing machine. Line up the outside edge of the foot with the raw edges of the fabric and machine along the entire length. Do not back stitch at the end of the row. Press the seams to one side.
3 When the required numbers of strips have been joined together, cut the band of fabric into equal lengths. You can then sew these small pieces together, staggering them so that a new pattern is formed. Carefully press each seam to one side.

Design suggestions

For more design ideas, there are many excellent books on Seminole patchwork (see the Bibliography, page 92).

If you want to experiment, you could incorporate ribbon or ricrac braiding, or automatic machine stitchery. These should be worked before the strips are cut up and rearranged.

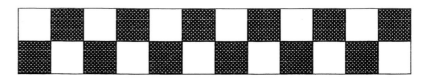

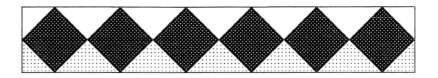

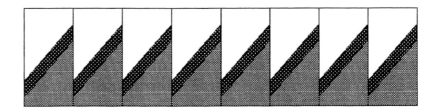

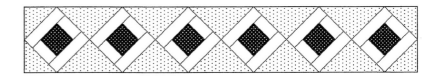

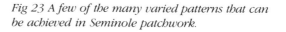

Fig 23 A few of the many varied patterns that can be achieved in Seminole patchwork.

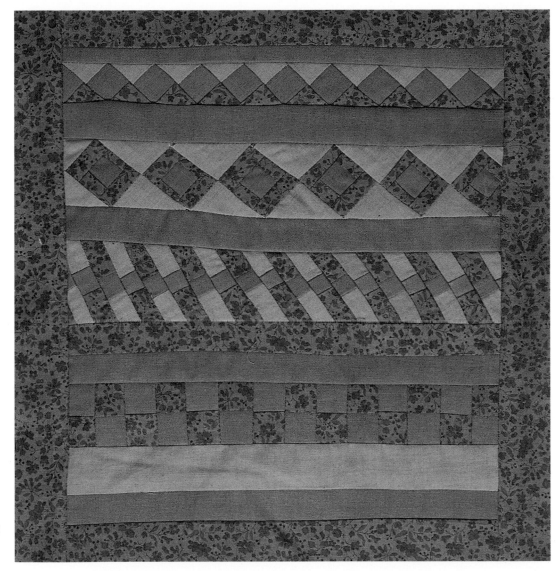

Seminole patchwork sample worked in plain and printed cottons, all dyed in tea (see page 20). (Jenny Bullen)

STRIP PATCHWORK

This is a natural development from Seminole patchwork and can lead to much experimentation. Unlike Log Cabin, which can be worked just as easily by hand, strip patchwork must be worked by machine as all the seams will be cut up and re-stitched and hand-sewn seams would not be strong enough.

(Above) *Design for a tote bag, with the initial letter 'T' worked in strip patchwork in a variety of cotton fabrics.*   (Margaret Rivers)

(Left) *Strip patchwork panel with strips of tie-dyed and patterned fabrics in a design based on diamonds.*   (Anne Coleman)

Method of working
Strip patchwork is very simple.

1 Cut strips of different fabrics and seam them together, as in the method of joining Log Cabin strips (Fig 24).
2 The resulting fabric can then be cut again into strips and re-seamed until the desired effect is achieved.

There are no real rules to be observed except to press all seam allowances together and press each seam as it is sewn. Try to avoid having too many bulky seams in the same place.

Design suggestions
Strips of equal lengths can be seamed together to provide effective borders for other types of patchwork, for instance Log Cabin (Fig 25). Try varying the widths of each strip to give more interest but beware of distracting attention from the quilt itself.

Strip patchwork can be cut into squares, triangles or other shapes to be used as an integral part of block patchwork. Do not restrict yourself to cottons or cotton blends. Experiment with dyed and painted fabrics, and with silks, satins, velvets, etc. Use an assortment of different fabrics that have all been dyed together (see page 19).

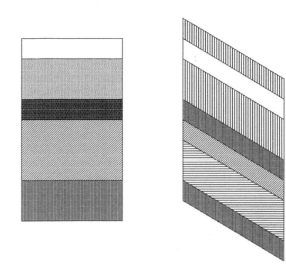

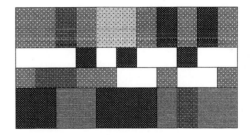

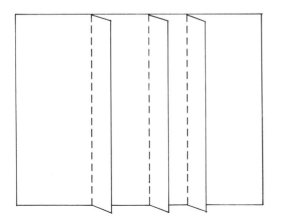

(Above) *Fig 25 Designs for strip patchwork are created by seaming a variety of different fabrics together, cutting them up and rearranging them to form new designs.*

(Left) *Fig 24 Machine stitch all the seams in strip patchwork with a 6 mm ($\frac{1}{4}$ in) seam allowance. Press each seam carefully on the wrong side with the turnings together.*

Strip patchwork using assorted fabrics, including velvets that have been dyed and overprinted. Extra surface decoration has been added with piped fabrics and machine embroidery. (Rosie Moore)

Cushion in strip patchwork, using plain and hand-dyed silks and cottons. Folded Star patches have been inserted in some of the seams. (Linda Cook)

To give added interest, insert Folded Star patches into the seams before joining the strips together. Ribbon and lace could also be used in the same way. Experiment with strips of fabric with frayed edges, or edges cut with pinking shears. (This method is not recommended for anything that will require a great deal of wear.) Alternatively, you could tuck or pleat a piece of fabric (this works very well if the fabric is random-dyed or hand-painted), then cut the fabric up into smaller units and rejoin them so that the tucks are placed in different directions.

In this sample, strips of assorted hand-dyed fabrics have been machined together, cut into four equal sections and rejoined. (Diana Mitchell)

BLOCK PATCHWORK

In this technique, small patches of fabric — squares and triangles — are seamed together in a particular sequence to form a design. These larger squares of fabric are called 'blocks'. Several blocks are then joined together to form a hanging or quilt. When the blocks are all sewn together, further patterns appear across the surface.

Many of these designs originated in Europe and were taken to North America by the early settlers. There they were given names such as Broken Dishes, Yankee Puzzle, Shoo Fly and Martha Washington's Star (Figs 26 and 27).

These blocks can all be seamed by hand and, indeed, that is how they were originally made. But with accurate cutting and careful seaming they can also be made very quickly on the time-saving sewing machine.

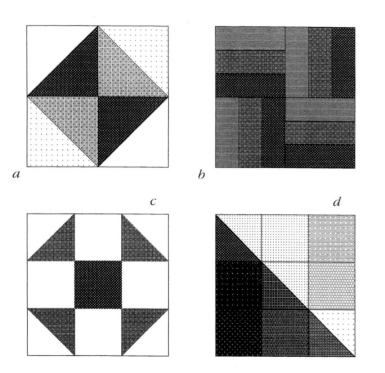

Fig 26 Four traditional block patterns. (a) Broken Dishes. (b) Roman Stripe. (c) Shoo Fly. (d) Nine-Patch.

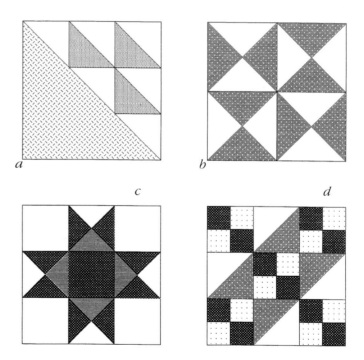

Fig 27 Four more traditional block patterns. (a) Birds in Air. (b) Yankee Puzzle. (c) Martha Washington's Star. (d) Road to California.

Making the templates

1 First choose a design. Select a simple one to start with, such as Shoo Fly. Decide on the size of your finished block. This can vary from 23 cm (9 in) to 40 cm (16 in) or even larger, although 30 cm (12 in) is a good size.

2 Draw the block to the correct size on a sheet of graph paper.

Carefully cut each shape and reserve one of each different component to make a template (Fig 28).

3 Glue each of the shapes onto thin, firm card. (Fine sandpaper can be used as an alternative; it provides a useful non-slip surface when placed on the fabric.) Add a 6 mm ($\frac{1}{4}$ in) seam allowance to each edge, then carefully cut out each template on the seamline (Fig 29).

Fig 28 Choose a suitable block (in this case Shoo Fly) and the required size. Draw the block to the correct size on a sheet of graph paper. Carefully cut out each shape and reserve one of each different component to use as a template.

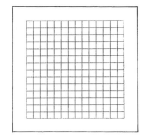

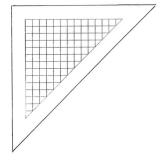

Fig 29 Carefully glue each shape onto thin, firm card or sandpaper. Add a 6 mm ($\frac{1}{4}$ in) seam allowance, then cut out each template on the seamline.

Cutting out the fabric

1 Choose the fabrics for your block. If this is your first attempt, it is best to use cotton. You will probably need no more than three or four different fabrics, and for Shoo Fly you only need two good contrasts. Press the fabric and lay it on a smooth, flat surface.

2 Count the number of patches required in each colour and make a note of them. (This is particularly important if you intend to make a large number of blocks.)

3 Place the card template on the fabric and carefully draw round the edge of each shape. Make sure that one straight edge is aligned with the straight grain of the fabric (Fig 30).

4 Cut out each fabric patch on the seamline. Do not add any extra seam allowance.

5 When you have cut out all the patches, arrange them on a flat surface to make the finished design (Fig 31).

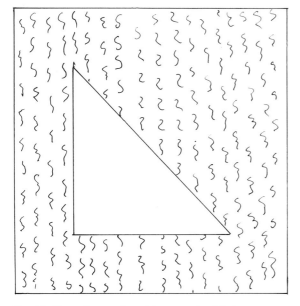

Fig 30 Place the card template on the fabric, making sure that one edge of the template is on the straight grain. (In the case of triangles, this should not be a diagonal edge.) Draw round the edge of each shape and cut out on this seamline. Do not add any extra seam allowance.

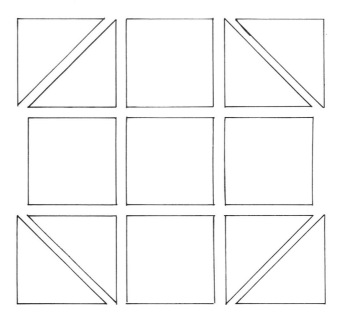

Fig 31 When all the patches have been cut out, arrange them on a board or flat surface to make up the design of the finished block.

Quilt based on a simple nine-patch block. Cotton fabrics, machine-pieced and hand-quilted.
(Sandra Hoult)

Joining the pieces

1 The pieces must be joined together in the correct sequence. Machine the smaller units (such as two triangles that will form a square) first and press the seams. Join the units that form a row, then stitch the rows together to make up the square.

2 Place the patches right sides together, with the raw edges matching. Pin them together, with the pins placed at right angles to the fabric (Fig 32a). If the patches are pinned in this way, the pins can be machined over without breaking the machine needle. The pins are then removed after the seam has been machined.

3 Place the patches in the machine so that the edge of the foot lines up with the raw edges of the fabric and machine them together (Fig 32b). If you use your machine foot as a seam guide in this way, there

Fig 32 To join the patches together, join the smaller units first of all. (a) Place two patches right sides together and pin, placing the pins at right angles to the fabric. (b) Place the fabric in the machine so that the edge of the foot lines up with the raw edges of the fabric. Machine each seam in turn. Do not back stitch at the beginning and end of each row. (c) Press the seam with the seam allowances together.

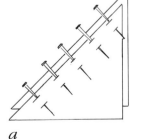

a

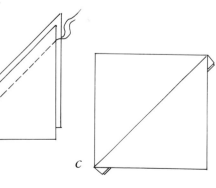

b

c

(Above) *Cushion in cotton fabrics. Machine-pieced and machine-quilted, using a decorative machine embroidery stitch.* (Rita Clark)

is no need to mark the seam on the fabric. Do not back stitch at the beginning or end of each row.

4 Press the seam with the seam allowances together (Fig 32c).

5 When joining the rest of the patches, take great care to ensure that the seams match up and that the points of the triangles match.

6 When each block is finished, press well and snip off all the ends of the sewing thread. If you are making several blocks, check that they are all the same size.

7 Place the blocks on a flat surface and arrange them in the finished design.

8 Machine the blocks together, carefully matching the seams. Make sure the blocks are all lying in the same direction.

Design suggestions

The possibilities for experimenting and designing are endless. You will probably find it easier and quicker to work on graph paper first before stitching. As well as graph paper, you will need lead pencils, a ruler and some coloured pencils.

It is a good idea to choose one block and to carry out as many different ideas as possible before moving on. You can achieve many individual and effective designs in this way. It provides a discipline to work within and eliminates some decision-making. Start with a simple block — Broken Dishes, one of the most basic, is extremely versatile. Work some traditional blocks but use dyed, hand-painted or printed fabrics.

Bag made for carrying a quilt, designed from traditional sources. Machine-pieced and hand-quilted in cotton fabrics. (Sandra Hoult)

By altering the traditional shading of each block, a quite different design will appear (Fig 33). Draw several blocks on graph paper, using this new design. You will find that new patterns can be formed with very little effort.

Fig 33 By altering the shading of parts of each block (in this case, Shoo Fly) a variety of different designs can be formed.

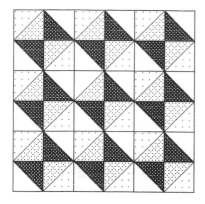

(Right) *Panel using patchwork as a design source. Hand-dyed silk patches glued to a background and held in place with stitchery. Silk and paper patches are used in the border.* (Anne Coleman)

(Left) *Scrap quilt using an assortment of cotton fabrics arranged carefully to form a striking design. Machine-pieced and hand-quilted.* (Pat Hooker)

Change the shape of the block (Fig 34). Instead of drawing a regular grid, make it irregular, with some of the squares quite small and others much larger. Work each variation to create some new, very original designs. Choose one and repeat it several times on graph paper to see how the finished result will look (Fig 35). Arrange the new block in different ways to form new patterns. Set the blocks at half-drop repeats with plain squares between each block (Fig 36). Draw them on the diagonal instead of square. Set them alternately with another block design.

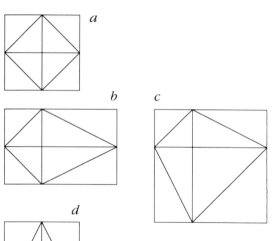

a

b

c

d

Fig 34 New blocks can be obtained by changing the size of different sections of traditional blocks. (a) Shoo Fly in its traditional, symmetrical form. (b–d) Variations of Shoo Fly, achieved by altering different sections within the basic block.

(Left) *Small hanging using dyed fabrics and embellished with embroidery stitches. Machine pieced and hand quilted.* (Jenny Bullen)

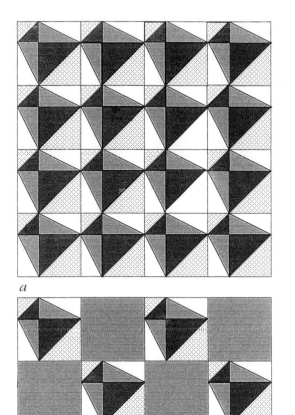

a

b

Fig 35 Experiments with the block illustrated in
Fig 34(c).
(a) The new block drawn out several times.
(b) The same block set with plain squares between
each block.

Fig 36 The block illustrated in Fig 35 set at half-
drop repeats for a wall hanging design. A small
component of the original block makes a simple
border pattern.

Instead of using ordinary graph paper, plot your own, using an irregular grid (Fig 37). It could have small squares at the centre (or slightly off-centre), radiating to larger squares or rectangles at the outer edges, or the other way round. Draw in the block design, carefully following each square.

Fig 37 An irregular grid used instead of ordinary graph paper. Broken Dishes has again been used as the design source.

Wall hanging based on the Kaleidoscope block. Worked entirely in cotton fabrics, machine-pieced and hand-quilted. (Jenny Bullen)

Detail of 'Square Dance Charm'.
(Ann Ohlenschlager)

Take several photocopies of the design you prefer so that you can experiment with different colourways. Try contrasts of colour, or toning or matching colours. Blend the colours across the design, from light to dark or from one colour to another. Starting at the centre of the design, radiate the colours from dark to light or from light to dark.

'Square Dance Charm'. A quilt in which no two patches are in the same fabric. A glorious array of fabrics carefully arranged to produce an eye-catching design. Machine-pieced and machine-quilted. (Ann Ohlenschlager)

Designing with computers

If you have access to a computer which will produce patterns, do make use of it. Much of the paperwork involved in designing quilts can be eliminated. Traditional blocks can be used or you can design totally new computer-orientated patterns (Fig 38). Practice is needed, of course, but exciting designs often appear by accident.

Paint programmes are now available for most computers although a 'mouse' is usually required, together with a high-quality screen suitable for graphics. If you are doubtful about the suitability of your machine you should consult your computer supplier. These programmes are usually operated by icons, small diagrams which give instructions, thus eliminating much of the jargon used by computer programmers.

Each stage of the work can be saved as a separate design, and these can then be worked on further. For instance, blocks can be rotated or new patterns overlaid. By using the mouse and clicking on different icons, you can make a range of marks. With the pencil icon, a single line is drawn across the screen. It is also possible to airbrush, paint and spatter marks. Any part of the design can be rubbed out by clicking on the eraser. Squares, polygons and some curved shapes can also be drawn, and it is possible to shade the design in a variety of different patterns very quickly.

Fig 38 Design for a small wall hanging using a computer. Rectangles, squares and triangles were drawn, duplicated and rotated until a suitable design was achieved.

(Right) *A small hanging based on the computer-aided design in Fig 38. Worked in Thai silks. Machine-pieced and hand-quilted.* (Jenny Bullen)

4

QUILTING AND FINISHING

Most of the projects illustrated in this book have been quilted. It is not always necessary to quilt patchwork but it offers several advantages. Warmth is a priority if you are making a bed quilt, and quilting gives a further dimension to the fabric surface, adding considerably to the finished design. There is also something very satisfying and comforting about quilting.

Wall hangings, cushions, etc. need not be quilted but you still need to consider the finish at the design stage. The patchwork could be stitched directly to a backing fabric, or simply quilted, either by hand or machine, through two layers of fabric (i.e. without wadding).

MATERIALS FOR QUILTING

A good backing fabric is essential for it will have as much wear and tear as the top fabric. Good-quality sheeting is ideal; it is available in wider widths than dress fabrics, which avoids the necessity of joining several lengths together. The fabric can be either plain or printed, but it should match the colour scheme of the quilt. Always wash and press the backing fabric before it is used.

For the wadding, choose a good-quality 2 oz wadding, available from specialist quilt shops (see Guide to Suppliers, page 93). If the finished article is to be washed, make sure that the wadding is also washable. If a flatter quilted appearance is required, domette (available from furnishing fabric departments) can be used, or even a flannelette sheet or an old, thin blanket.

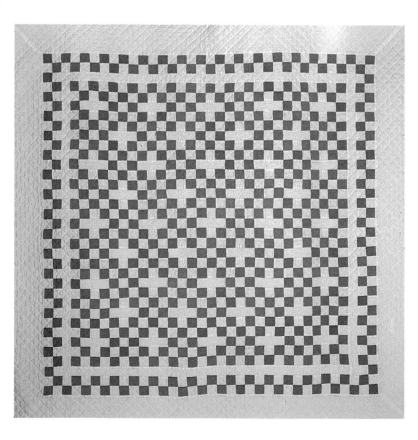

82

(Right) *The design for this quilt was influenced by Indian patchwork. It has been hand-quilted in a variety of coloured threads so that the quilting pattern plays an important part in the surface design.* (Jean Draper)

(Left) *Irish Chain quilt in cotton fabrics, machine-pieced and beautifully hand-quilted.* (Sandra Hoult)

You will also need tacking thread, 'betweens' (or quilting) needles, pins, small scissors, a thimble and quilting thread. Special quilting thread is now obtainable at quilt supply shops. Alternatively, use a strong sewing cotton (one that contains polyester is probably best). Choose a colour that blends with, or is slightly darker than, the colours in the patchwork. A piece of beeswax is also useful to run the sewing thread through; it helps to strengthen the thread. Quilting hoops are helpful but not essential, and some quilters like to use a full-size frame.

QUILTING DESIGNS

Many people prefer to follow the lines of their patchwork as they quilt and this makes a perfectly acceptable design. However, a quilting design does not have to follow the work at all; curved lines of quilting that sweep across the surface give a great feeling of movement. If you have plain areas of fabric in the patchwork, you can fill them with individual quilting motifs — flowers, or a geometric pattern, or one of the traditional quilting patterns that are still in use today (Fig 39).

Whatever quilting pattern you use, you need to give careful thought to the overall design quite early on as complicated quilting patterns must be transferred to the quilt top before the fabrics are sandwiched together. You can buy stencils for marking complicated patterns (see Guide to Suppliers, page 93), or make your own design using thin card.

There are several different marking tools available and it is advisable to try out different methods on scrap fabric. Many quilters prefer a well-sharpened B or HB pencil. Water-soluble marking pens should be used with great care as they have a habit of returning after they have been washed out, and it is now generally agreed that the chemicals in them could harm the fabric. Water-soluble crayons are worth investigating.

The traditional method of needlemarking is still very successful, although it can only be used just before quilting as the line will fade away. Place the stencil on the quilt surface and draw firmly round it with a large darning needle.

PREPARING THE FABRIC

1 When the patchwork has been completed it should be pressed, preferably with a steam iron, and all thread ends carefully snipped away. It is useful, too, at this stage, to check for mistakes in the design, something that is not easily rectified after quilting.

2 Cut the backing fabric to size (ideally slightly larger than the finished patchwork). If it has to be joined, remove all the selvedges and machine the seams together. Press the seams open. Lay the fabric on a flat surface (a table top or floor).

3 Cut the wadding to the correct size. This often has to be joined to achieve the correct width. To do this, carefully butt the two edges together and oversew them with large stitches. Lay the wadding over the backing fabric, removing any loose threads that may have appeared and smoothing out any bumps or ridges.

4 Lay the top over the wadding, smoothing it in place.

5 Beginning at the centre of the quilt, tack the centre vertical and horizontal lines, stitching through all three layers. Then tack parallel lines over the whole quilt to make a grid (Fig. 40). The tacking lines should never be more than 10 cm (4 in) apart; they will keep the three layers together during the quilting process and prevent the fabrics from becoming creased. Hand-quilting takes a considerable amount of time, so it is worth spending a little time on the preparation.

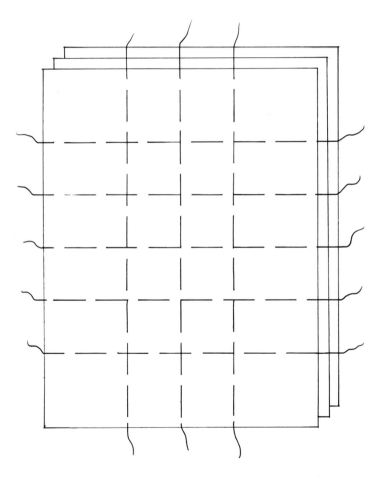

(Left) *Fig 39 A few of the many traditional quilting patterns.*

Fig 40 Preparing the fabrics for quilting. Press the backing fabric and lay it on a flat surface. Smooth the wadding in place. Press the top fabric and lay it carefully on top of the wadding. Beginning at the centre, tack a grid of horizontal and vertical lines, approximately 10 cm (4 in) apart.

STITCHING

1 If you intend to use a quilting hoop, place the centre of the quilt in the hoop. Unlike embroidery, where the fabric must be drum-tight, the three layers should be held firmly together but not stretched too tightly. It should be possible to work several stitches at a time without any difficulty.

2 Thread the needle with quilting thread (never have too long a thread) and make a small knot in the end. Begin stitching in the centre of the quilt and work evenly from this point out to the edges.

3 To commence stitching, take the needle through the top fabric only a short distance from the starting point (Fig 41). Give a short, sharp tug on the thread and the knot should disappear under the top fabric. (Sometimes the knot will break and it may be necessary to repeat this stage.) No knots or finishing should appear on the backing fabric.

4 The stitch used for quilting is nearly always running stitch (Fig 42), especially on larger pieces of work when other stitches such as back stitch are not feasible. Aim to keep the length of the stitches and the spaces in between them as even as possible. Do not worry about the size of the stitches (the more quilting you do, the smaller your stitches will be). It should be possible to work several stitches at a time. As you pull the threads through the fabrics, pull slightly on the thread (do not tug or the thread will weaken and break).

5 To finish off, bring the needle up through the last stitch made, actually piercing the thread (Fig 43). Take the needle through the top fabric only and bring it out a short distance away. Snip off the thread end.

Fig 41 To commence quilting, thread the needle and make a small knot at the end of the thread. Take the needle through the fabric a short distance from the starting point. Give a short, sharp tug on the thread and the knot will disappear.

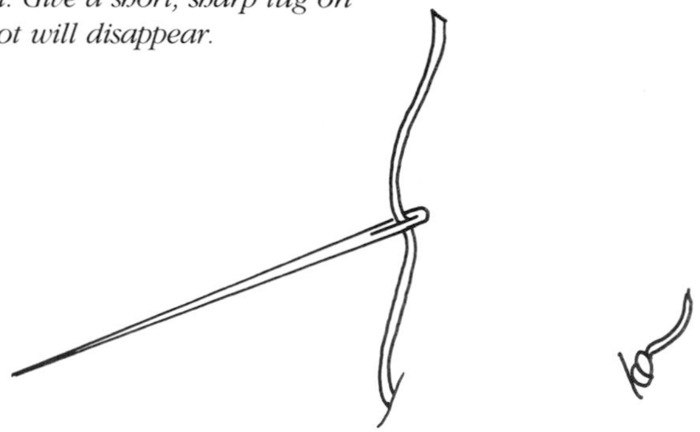

Fig 42 Running stitch is most often used for quilting. With practice, it should be possible to work several stitches at a time before pulling the needle through the fabric.

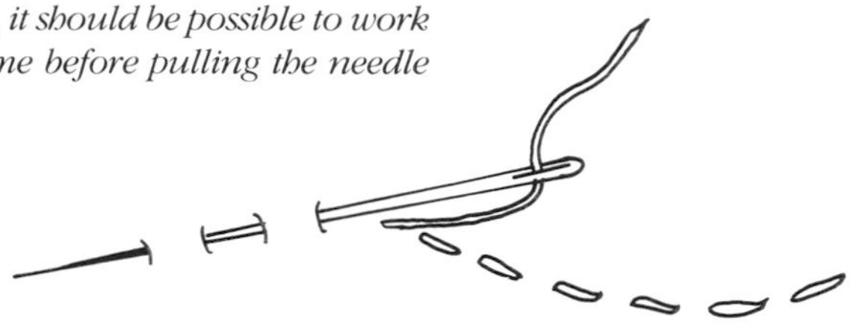

Fig 43 To finish off, bring the needle up through the centre of the last stitch made so that it actually pierces the thread. Take the needle through the top fabric only and bring it out a short distance away, then snip off the end of the thread.

TIED QUILTS

If it is not possible or desirable to quilt a piece of work, tied knots are a much speedier process. Use a strong thread such as buttonhole thread; a thicker wadding than 2 oz can be used if required. Prepare the fabrics as before. Thread a needle and, at regular intervals over the surface, take the needle down through all the layers and bring it up again in the same spot leaving a length of thread on the surface. Repeat and then tie a reef knot on the surface before cutting the thread, leaving ends of approximately 3 cm (1 in) (Fig 44).

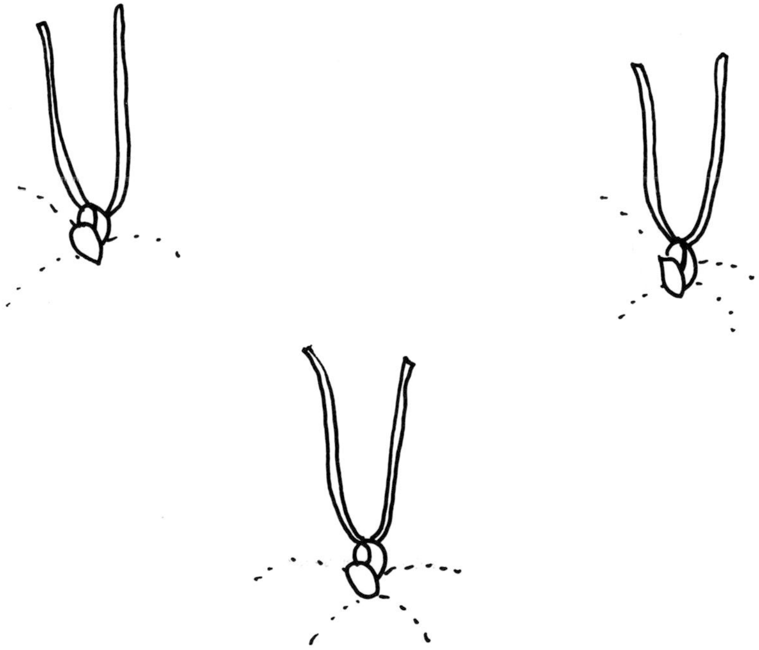

Fig 44 To tie-quilt, the fabric should first be prepared as for quilting. Tie reef knots at regular intervals across the surface. Cut the threads, leaving ends of approximately 3 cm (1 in). (If the ends of the knots are any shorter, they will soon unravel.)

QUILT-AS-YOU-GO

This method is often used by quilters who do not wish, or are unable, to work on a large area of fabric at a time. Each block is quilted separately and the blocks sewn together at the end.

When each block is finished, it should be pressed well. Make a sandwich of squares of backing, wadding and top fabric, then tack and quilt each square before joining them all together (Fig 45a).

To join the blocks, place two blocks right sides together and pin so that the points of each block meet. Machine together the top fabrics and wadding only (Fig 45b). Trim the wadding and neaten the raw edges. Turn under one raw edge of the backing fabric so that it covers the other raw edge and hem stitch neatly in place (Fig 45c).

Fig 45 Quilt-as-you-go is a method of finishing a quilt or wall hanging in which each individual block is quilted and then the blocks sewn together
(a) Press each block and make a sandwich of backing fabric, wadding and top fabric. Quilt the blocks in the desired design.
(b) To join the blocks, place two blocks right sides together and machine through the top fabrics and wadding only. Trim the wadding and the seam allowances on the top fabrics.
(c) On the back of the quilt, turn under one raw edge of the backing fabric and hem stitch neatly in place.

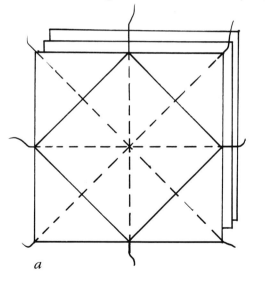

a

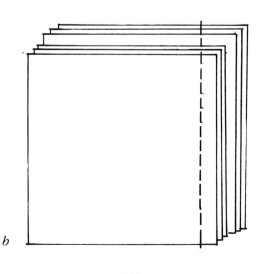

b

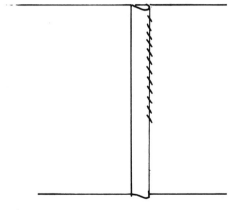

c

BINDING

When the patchwork top has been completed, the edges may need to be bound. Neaten and trim away all excess fabric around the edges. Usually one of the fabrics in the patchwork is chosen for the binding, but this is a matter for individual choice.

1 Cut strips approximately 4 cm (1½ in) wide on the straight grain of the fabric. (It is not necessary to cut bias strips unless the edges of the quilt are curved.) Join the strips together to obtain the correct length.
2 With the right sides together and the raw edges matching, pin the binding to the quilt. Machine through all the layers (Fig 46a).
3 Turn the binding to the wrong side, turn under the seam allowance and hand stitch to the backing fabric (Fig 46b).

HANGING WORK

If a wall hanging or quilt is to be displayed at an exhibition, make a fabric sleeve on the wrong side through which you can insert a pole or baton.

Cut a strip of fabric the width of the quilt and approximately 12 cm (5 in) deep. Fold it in half and machine the seams together to form a tube. Turn to the right side. Turn in the raw edges on the two short sides and slip stitch in place. Pin the sleeve to the top of the quilt and hem the two long ends to the backing fabric.

Always remember to sign and date your work.

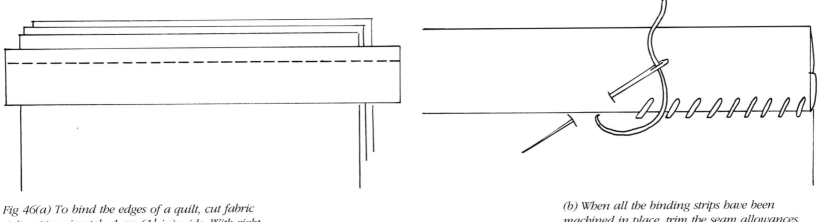

Fig 46(a) To bind the edges of a quilt, cut fabric strips approximately 4 cm (1½ in) wide. With right sides together and raw edges matching, pin and then stitch the binding to the quilt.

(b) When all the binding strips have been machined in place, trim the seam allowances. Fold the binding to the back of the quilt, turn under the raw edge and hand stitch in place.

CLEANING AND CARING FOR QUILTS

If all the fabrics used in the project are washable, bed quilts can be washed carefully by hand in the bath using warm water and pure soap flakes. Rinse very carefully to remove all traces of soap and leave to dry, preferably on a flat surface.

If the fabrics used are not washable (i.e. silks or hand-dyed or hand-painted fabrics) then the quilt should ideally be dry-cleaned. Wall hangings can be dusted with a vacuum cleaner at regular intervals. Remember that the sun will cause some fabrics to fade and others to rot. Quilts and wall hangings should be placed in a position out of strong sunlight.

If you are fortunate enough to have an antique quilt, do not attempt to clean it until you have sought expert advice.

Detail of the quilt on page 83. The fabric around the central motif has been slashed to reveal other fabrics beneath. (Jean Draper)

BIBLIOGRAPHY

Vicki Barker and Tessa Bird, *The Fine Art of Quilting*, Studio Vista, 1990

Valerie Campbell-Harding, *Strip Patchwork*, B.T. Batsford Ltd, 1983

Cheryl Greider Bradkin, *The Seminole Patchwork Book*, Cheryl Greider Bradkin

Beth Gutcheon, *The Perfect Patchwork Primer*, Penguin Books, 1973

Jill Liddell and Yuko Watanabe, *Japanese Quilts*, Studio Vista, 1990

Judy Martin, *Patchwork*, Charles Scribner & Sons, 1983

Katie Pasquini, *The Contemporary Sampler*, Sudz Publishing, 1985

Michele Walker, *Quiltmaking in Patchwork and Appliqué*, Ebury Press, 1985

MAGAZINES

The Quilter, The Quilters' Guild OP66, Dean Clough, Halifax HX3 5AX

Patchwork and Quilting, 1 Highfield Close, Malvern Link, Worcestershire WR14 1SH

GUIDE TO SUPPLIERS

Barnyarns
Langrish
Nr Petersfield
Hampshire GU32 1RQ

Green Hill
27 Bell Street
Romsey
Hampshire SO51 8GY

The Patchwork Dog and Calico Cat
21 Chalk Farm Road
London NW1

The Quilt Room
20 West Street
Dorking
Surrey RH4 1BL

Pat Riches
18 Monks Orchard
Petersfield
Hampshire GU32 2JD

Strawberry Fayre
Chagford
Devon TQ13 8EN

Village Fabrics
30 Goldsmiths Lane
Oxon OX10 ODN

George Weil and Sons Ltd
18 Hanson Street
London W1P 7DB

(Warehouse)
Reading Arch Road
Redhill
Surrey RH1 1HG

INDEX